JOHN THOMPSON RECITAL SERIES

Intermediate to Advanced

SPIRITUALS

6 GREAT ARRANGEMENTS BY JOHN THOMPSON

ISBN 978-1-4803-9966-2

WILLIS MUSIC

EXCLUSIVELY DISTRIBUTED BY

HAL•LEONARD®
CORPORATION
7777 W. BLUEMOUND RD. P.O. BOX 13819
MILWAUKEE, WISCONSIN 53213

© 2015 by The Willis Music Co.
International Copyright Secured   All Rights Reserved

Visit Hal Leonard Online at
www.halleonard.com

Deep River

Spiritual
Arranged by John Thompson

Heav'n, Heav'n

Spiritual
Arranged by John Thompson

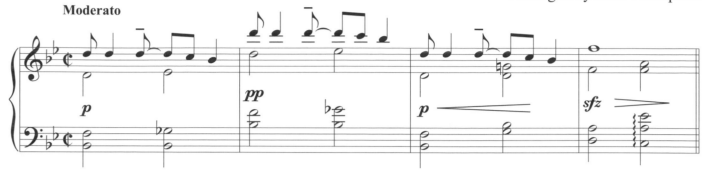

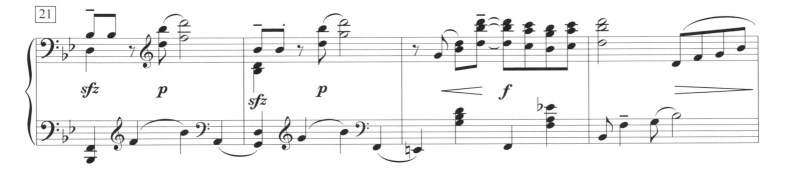

Maestoso

I Want to Be Ready
(Walk in Jerusalem, Jus' Like John)

Spiritual
Arranged by John Thompson

Andante moderato

With pedal

Nobody Knows de Trouble I've Seen

Spiritual
Arranged by John Thompson

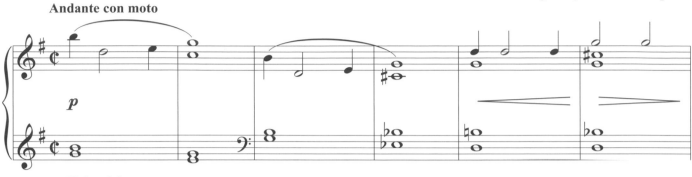

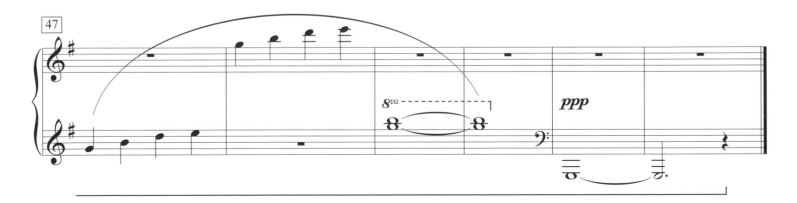

Swing Low, Sweet Chariot

Spiritual
Arranged by John Thompson

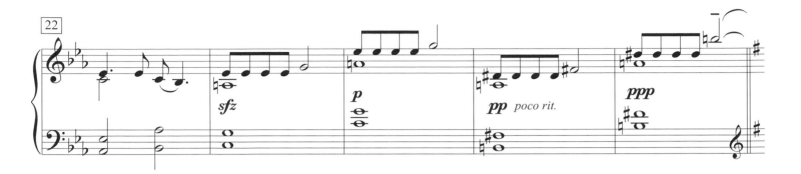

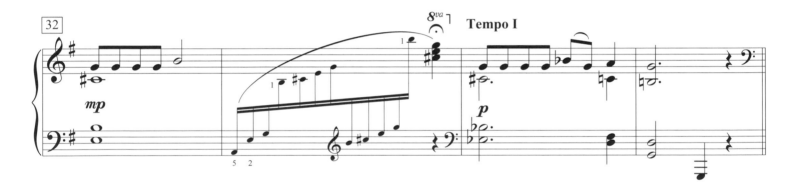

Short'nin' Bread

Spiritual
Arranged by John Thompson

Allegro brillante

Più moderato

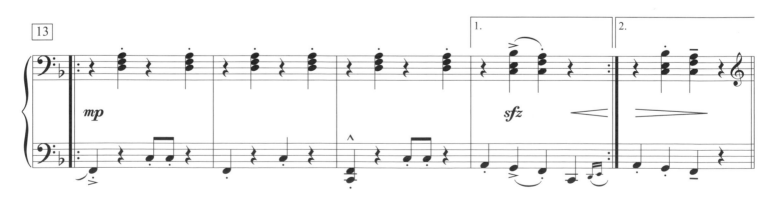

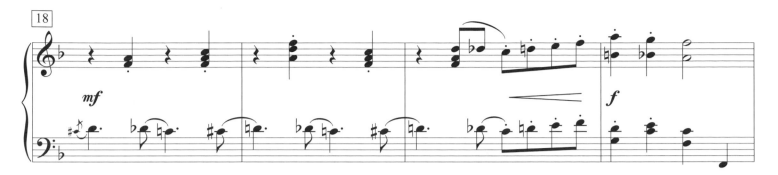

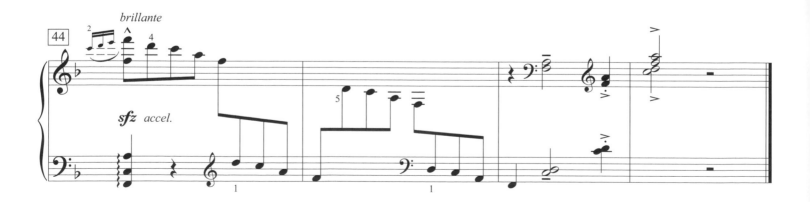